# AFFIRMATIONS

## FOR

# BETTER LIVING

Positive Self-Talk for a Happier,
Healthier, Wealthier, Wiser YOU!

## By Kalimba Love

*Interior Photography: Kalimba Love

*Exceptions:
Sets 6, 13 & 31-Samm, Set 26-Alexander Glinton
Back Cover-David Torrella

Published by
Kalimba Love Enterprises
OHM Publishing Division

www.kalimbalove.com
Ask@kalimbalove.com

# Here's what others are saying about this book...

### Powerful life changing affirmations, a must read—5 Stars
I literally couldn't put this book down. It exudes simplicity, yet is full of life altering suggestions.

You'll discover some incredibly beautiful photos among the pages which support the statements you read.

On the whole I found this book very inspirational.

I absolutely recommend this book to everyone so they can discover the transformative power of affirmative prayers. They have the power to let you experience more love, joy, peace of mind and passion into your life. This book is a must have for your library! –*Henry Garman*

### A Self-Healing Tool – 5 Stars
This book is a great tool to create a meditation and affirmation practice anywhere you may be. The affirmations attune you to your best self and free you from your limitations. The images of nature, animals, and people remind us to look for the joy and peace all around us. A "must have" in your library! –*SoulSong*

### Superb Book/Superb Reading – 5 Stars
I thought I would only read a chapter at a time...I literally couldn't put it down. Easy to read and easy to follow, the author was clear, concise and used practical examples throughout. Filled with life-altering suggestions and great ideas that are easy to follow and implement.

I give it two thumbs up. Had the scale gone up higher, I would have given it more stars. –*Professor*

### Beautifully Done! – 5 Stars
This book is beautifully and exquisitely done. It exudes simplicity. The photos seem to support the statements in some subtle, subconscious way. Usually, I feel skeptical or overwhelmed by books on affirmations. This book leaves me feeling accepting and convinced that I can do it, whatever "it" is. –*annabethK*

### A powerful tool to improve the quality of your life – 5 Stars
The author has crafted a powerful book filled with light. The reader can take the journey to a better understanding of life and how it works by using the affirmations presented. This material is powerful and can help you transform your life and those around you if you choose to use this material. The photos add another dimension to this material and help focus on the true beauty that life is about. –*D. Waisner*

# Gratitude & Appreciation

*To the memory of my father, I. Victor Yancey*
*My mother, Ida M. Yancey-Wilson*
*My brother, Gregory M. Johnson*
*My grandson, Kojo Sa-Ra*

This book would not be in your hands if it were not for some very special people in my life who inspired and/or contributed in some way to help me get it done.

I am so grateful for the love and support of these Beautiful Blessings and want to acknowledge them for being instrumental in accomplishing this Labor of Love and helping me to move this project from "vision" to reality!

THANK YOU to GOD—The Great Life Force & Divine Creator of ALL that IS; my Beloved Sons—Christopher, Jashua & Marques; all my Grandchildren; my mother—Ida Shaw Yancey; my brothers—Greg Johnson & Jonathon Yancey; my sister-Allyson McCalister; my father—I. Victor Yancey; Rev. Michael Bernard Beckwith & Ricki Byars-Beckwith; BarbaraO; Nancy Caldwell; Alma Turner; my COLC Family; Taylor Stevens; Ken Williamson; Kevin Ross; Vic Johnson; Diane & Michael Rivers; Diana Loy; Marijah; Regina Wilson; Johanna Cassidy; Renee Smith; Regina Davis; Eunice Louis-Ferdinand; Russell Brame; Nantambu Ahota; Alexander Glinton; Paul "JP" Jones; Renee McClendon; my Designer Life Mastermind Partners; Cordelia Jones; my PC Professor friends—Corey, Christy, Rob & Howard Fellman, David & Gissela Torrella; Quetel "Que" Osterval & the staff of Ugo Print; and the following artists, authors, and teachers who have inspired & encouraged me throughout the years: Minnie Riperton, Stevie Wonder, Maurice White, Michael Jackson, Dr. Robert H. Schuler, Vera Stanley Alder, Deepak Chopra, Dr. Joseph Murphy, Ernest Holmes, James Allen, Bruce Muzik, and so many more, whom I don't have room to name. Heartfelt thanks to ALL of you who have contributed your Love & Wisdom to the person I AM!

# Introduction

(By The Author)

**These Tools for Transformation WILL change Your Life!** Using these affirmations has made a Tremendous Difference in my Outlook and Experience of Life! Before I started writing and using positive affirmative prayers, my negative programming and self-talk kept me locked in clinical depression and in a constant struggle with day-to-day living. There were so many creative urges pushing me to DO more, BE more, HAVE more—yet I seemed powerless to Stay Focused on anything long enough to make it happen.

This book, now in its 4th publishing, is direct evidence of the Transformative Power of Affirmative Prayer! This completed Master Mind Project debuted in October of 2011 and has continued to evolve hand-in-hand with the Open Heart Ministry (OHM) Family, of which I am the co-founder and spiritual director.

Alignment with these affirmations WILL bring out the BEST In You. It is my sincere desire that you will use these affirmative prayers to change the voices inside your head into your best friends and cheerleaders, thus empowering you to transform your life into the Stellar Experience the Creator has in mind for you!

If you desire to experience *More Love, More Joy, More Confidence, More Power, More Passion, and More Prosperity* in your life, using these affirmations *WILL* help!

*Note: Most of the pictures were taken near my home in beautiful Lake Worth and Palm Beach, Florida. A few are from my travels to Hawaii, Los Angeles, and Ohio. The beauty I see all around my neighborhood contributes to my feeling of enjoying Heaven on Earth!

# Table of Contents

# How to USE This Book for Best Results

An affirmation is a declarative statement of truth. This volume includes **52 sets** of very powerful positive affirmations. The purpose is to recognize these words as your own Higher Truth as the Creator sees you. When you make these declarations, you **set forces into motion** that begin to **transform your mind**...and therefore, your attitude, and ultimately your actions and your outcomes.

There are **several effective ways** to use this book. I suggest that you browse through the entire book for your first reading, then modify your approach for regular use. I wrote and focused on one set of these affirmative prayers per week and found it to be quite effective in reprogramming my own self-talk. If you are new to this concept, after browsing through the entire book, I recommend focusing on **one set per week or one per day**. You might also choose a relevant topic from the Table of Contents for specific guidance as you need it. Some more advanced students choose to read the **entire book** as part of their morning ritual before going on to the rest of the day.

**Practice reading these affirmations out loud** with *feeling,* imagining how you would *feel* if they were true for you now. It is BEST to do this first thing in the morning or last thing at night. These are the times when our minds are most fertile and receptive.

At first it may feel awkward—like you're just telling lies, but **the repetition process begins to re-program your mind**. Then your mind begins to generate energy and ideas for how to bring your declarations into a living reality...and inspires the determination to follow them through to fulfillment. The old programs like "I'm not good enough" or "you'll never be able to make a living as an artist" begin to be replaced with programs like **"I can DO this! I KNOW I can!"**

It is only fair I should give you one warning: when you begin to affirm a Higher Truth, the Universe begins to send you "exercises" and "pop quizzes" to help you strengthen your spiritual "muscles." *So be prepared to have your resolve "tested"* so to speak. But don't let fear or procrastination steal your blessings! Just continue to pray with FAITH for the strength, courage, patience & perseverance to *LIVE the Best Life you can imagine!*

You are encouraged to use the ideas here to inspire you to write your own prayers, affirmations, and insights and to refer to them often.

*You are embarking on a New Life! Enjoy your journey!!!*

*Please note, I frequently use ABBA as a personal name for the Divine Masculine Aspect of God and AMMA for the Divine Feminine Aspect. Feel free to replace the names with your own personal Name(s) for God—the Great Life Force that is the Creative Force of the Universe.*

♡

I AM the LOVE that
God INTENDS me to be!

I AM GROWING and EVOLVING at
precisely the right time and space to BE
the BEST ME I can BE!

I AM WORTHY of ALL of the Gifts &
Blessings THIS LIFE has to offer
BECAUSE I AM LOVE!

♡

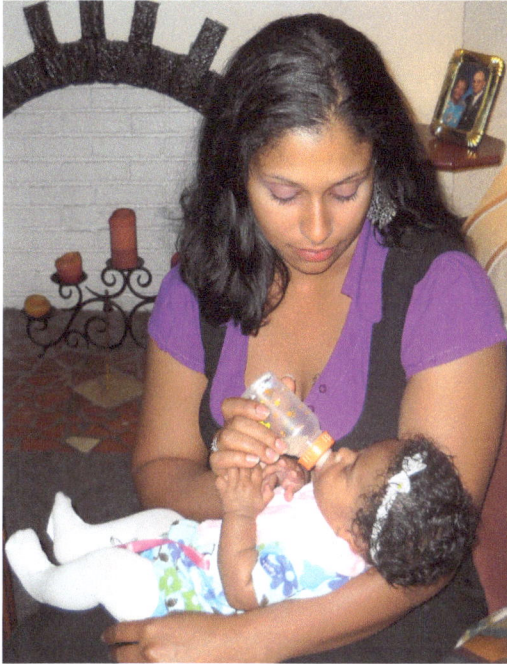

I Aᴍ a Loving Child of Goᴅ.

Goᴅ Is Loᴠᴇ…I Aᴍ Loᴠᴇ.

I Aᴍ Love, I Am Loved,
I Am Loving & I Am Lovable.

I Deserve to Love and to Be Loved.

I Aᴍ Worthy of Life's Blessings because
I Aᴍ a Loving Child of God.

I Deeply and Completely Accept &
Love Myself and Those Around Me.

1

I AM GRATEFUL for every beginning
and every ending of EVERY DAY.

I feel GRATITUDE and APPRECIATION for
EVERYONE and EVERYTHING blessing my life.

THANK YOU AMMA. THANK YOU ABBA for
clearing my VISION
and fine-tuning my sense of PURPOSE.

Thank YOU for ALL of the BLESSINGS
IN, THRU & AS my Life.

I process my emotions with
PATIENCE, LOVE, and COMPASSION.

THANK YOU for FREEING me from
guilt, shame, and blame.

THANK YOU for freeing me from
old anger and resentment.

THANK YOU for increasing my capacity for
LOVE, COMPASSION and UNDERSTANDING.

I RELEASE all pain and resentment
from my past and present.

Even though I've made mistakes in the past,
I DEEPLY and COMPLETELY
ACCEPT and LOVE MYSELF.

THANK YOU GOD for forgiving me for every
mistake and every shortcoming in my past.

I FORGIVE MYSELF and everyone I ever
perceived to have wronged me.

I AM AT PEACE within myself.

I Am the Love that
God Intends me to be!

I Am Growing and Evolving at
precisely the right time and space to Be
the Best Me I can Be!

I Am Worthy of All of the Gifts &
Blessings This Life has to offer
Because I Am Love!

Thank you for Healing
my Mind, my Heart and my Soul.

I Aᴍ a Unique Expression of
Divine Intelligence, Divine Beauty,
and Divine Love.

I Aᴍ willing to Bᴇʟɪᴇᴠᴇ that
I Aᴍ Pᴇʀꜰᴇᴄᴛ, Wʜᴏʟᴇ & Cᴏᴍᴘʟᴇᴛᴇ
in the Eʏᴇs and the Mɪɴᴅ of Gᴏᴅ!

My Mɪssɪᴏɴ and My Pᴜʀᴘᴏsᴇ are unfolding
with the Grace and Beauty of a Rose!

Thank Yᴏᴜ Aᴍᴍᴀ! Thank Yᴏᴜ Aʙʙᴀ!

I Cᴀɴ Dᴏ Tʜɪs! I Kɴᴏw I Cᴀɴ!

I Am God's Love In Action!

Thank you for creating a
Compassionate Heart in Me.

I am Compassionate and Patient
with myself and with others.

I listen compassionately and respond with
sensitivity when loved ones come to me for
comfort and encouragement.

GOD IS LOVE...I AM LOVE...

My life is filled with Loving Friendships.

Thank You for HEALING
ALL of My RELATIONSHIPS!

I Trust the LOVE of GOD as I Open my Heart.

I AM SO GRATEFUL for ALL of the
LOVE that fills & fulfills My Life!

Thank You ABBA...Thank You AMMA

I ALLOW a BEACON of SACRED LIGHT to shine
In, Thru & As My Life.

I RELEASE All Fear and ALLOW the
Love & the Light of God to Light My Way.

Thank You, ABBA, for clearing my VISION
and fine-tuning my sense of PURPOSE.

I AM the LIGHT.
It is my NATURE to SHINE.

All of my Relationships are Loving,
Harmonious, Joyful & Mutually Beneficial.
THANK YOU for
Healing my RELATIONSHIP with YOU!
THANK YOU for
Healing my RELATIONSHIP with ME!
THANK YOU for Healing my RELATIONSHIPS
with ALL of my FAMILY & FRIENDS.
Thank YOU for the LOVE, THE FUN & the JOY we share.

Thank You ABBA for the WAYS & MEANS of using my gifts, talents & skills at the TOPMOST LEVEL that is possible!

Thank You for DIRECTING my THOUGHTS, WORDS, ACTIONS and Environment quickly and easily to LOVE, JOY, PEACE, POWER & FULFILLMENT of my DREAMS, DESIRES, GOALS & PURPOSE!

Thank You for proving your LOVE for me EVERY DAY in EVERY WAY!

I TRUST YOU to BE ALL that I AM and ALL that I DESIRE!

I AM FREE of destructive emotional
responses and reactions!

I HONOR MY FEELINGS and process them with
PATIENCE, KINDNESS & COMPASSION.

THANK YOU, ABBA, for FREEING ME from the
pain, anger and resentment that
would destroy my body.

I Am So Grateful for the
PEACE, LOVE, JOY & PERFECT HEALTH
that come rushing in to take their place.

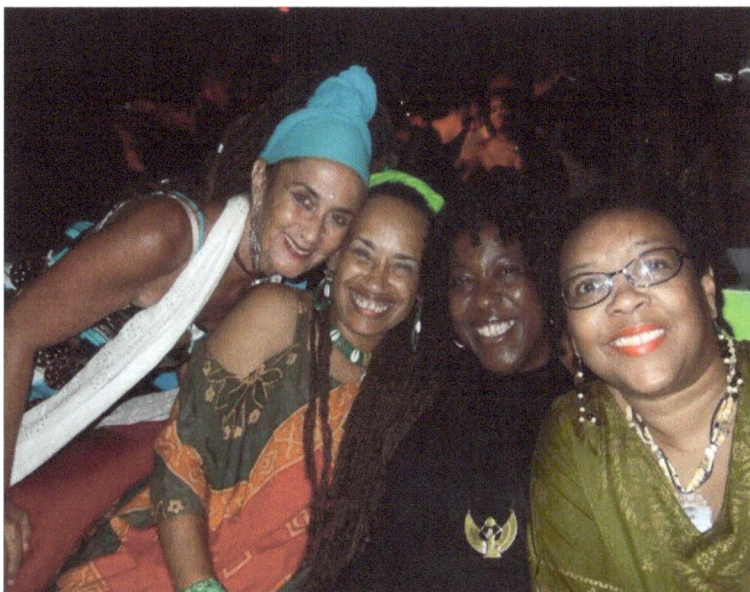

My life is FILLED with FUN, LOVE, JOY,
PEACE, POWER & PROSPERITY!

THANK YOU ABBA…Thank YOU AMMA,
for ALL of the BLESSINGS that ARE my LIFE!

Thank You for healing
ALL of my Relationships.

I LOVE and APPRECIATE the GOD in ME!

MY LIFE SHINES for all to see
the JOY, PEACE, POWER, PROSPERITY
& the FUN that are POSSIBLE with GOD IN ME!

THANK YOU for USING ME so powerfully as a
BEACON OF LIGHT on this Earth Plane!

I AM becoming the STRONG, SUCCESSFUL,
HAPPY, LOVING, and COMPASSIONATE person
I've always wanted to Be.

I AM a Manifest EXPRESSION of the LOVE,
the LIFE, the PEACE, the POWER, the PASSION,
& the JOY of GOD!

THANK YOU GOD, for CUSTOMIZING My LIFE
for YOUR HIGHEST & BEST GOOD!

Thank You for helping me to Focus my Thoughts, Time and Resources in the Direction of my Highest & Best Good!

Thank you for Channeling the myriad Gifts, Talents & Skills You have Blessed Me with in the Direction which most benefits You, Me, My Family, My Community & The World!

Thank You for Being the Source of All that I Am, All that I Have, All that I Give, and All that I Receive!

My VISION and PURPOSE are crystal clear.

I choose to *raise the vibrational level of my own being*, thereby raising the vibrational level *all around me*.

I create LOVE, BEAUTY, PEACE, & HARMONY every day for myself and my environment.

Thank you for ORGANIZING, VITALIZING & PRIORITIZING Every Aspect of my life!

THANK YOU So Much for MANIFESTING the DESIRES of my Heart in my HERE & NOW!

I AM Living my Custom Designed Life RIGHT NOW!

Thank YOU ABBA! Thank YOU AMMA!

Thank You for OPENING THE WAY
to Live and Teach SUCCESS PRINCIPLES and
for the PROSPERITY FOR ALL that results.

Thank you for the DRAMATICALLY
IMPROVED LIFESTYLES that result!

Thank You for UPLIFTING, MOTIVATING,
INSPIRING & EMPOWERING ME
and so many Others THRU ME!

I OPEN FULLY and SURRENDER to
my HIGHEST & BEST GOOD!

How can I PROSPER MYSELF, my FAMILY and my
COMMUNITY while using my Talents at the UTMOST
Level that is POSSIBLE?

Thank YOU for providing the increase in our family
HEALTH, WEALTH, JOY, LOVE & PEACE!

Thank YOU for Dramatically Improving our PROSPERITY
MANAGEMENT SKILLS!

I Am DIRECTED & GUIDED moment by moment on the PATH OF GREATEST GOOD!

I live my life Fully and Completely and accomplish my goals with ease and with joy.

I create an outward expression of the Beauty and Joy of Life in my Attitude, my Home, my Work, & my Environment.

THANK YOU GOD FOR USING ME in a Powerful, Beautiful & Loving Way To UPLIFT, MOTIVATE, INSPIRE & EMPOWER Everyone whose Lives I Touch.

PLEASE HELP ME & HELP MY FAMILY!

Help us to HEAL ALL the PAIN from our PAST
and to LOVE each other
Holistically and Happily.

Show us the WAY...Help us move into
a WHOLE and HAPPY sense of
SELF LOVE & SELF FORGIVENESS.

HELP ME to FORGIVE MYSELF and
EVERY member of my Family...and
HELP THEM to FORGIVE ME.

I FLOW FORWARD in Life with DIVINE ACTION.

THANK YOU for helping me to
TRUST YOU more & more and to
RELAX INTO YOUR LOVE!

THANK YOU for increasing my
FAITH & FOLLOW-THRU!

I RELEASE all guilt, fear, blame,
shame, judgment, and resentment.

I BREAK THROUGH ALL barriers TO SUCCESS.

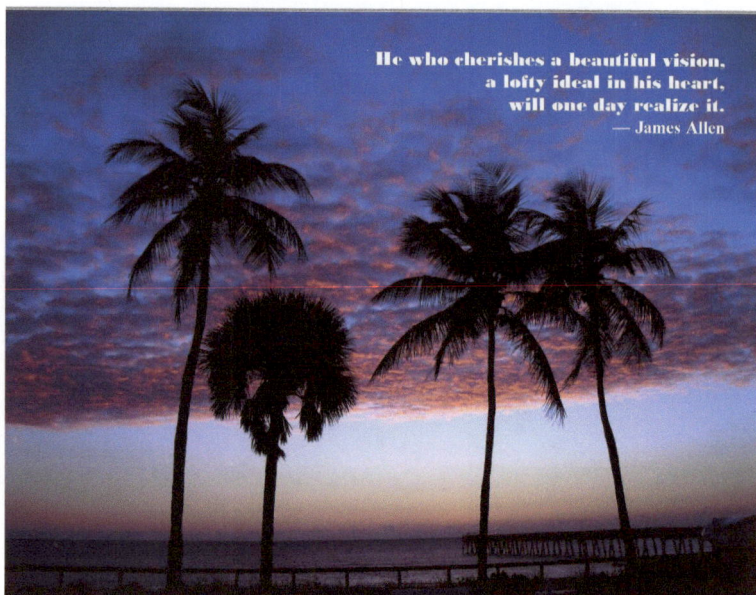

He who cherishes a beautiful vision,
a lofty ideal in his heart,
will one day realize it.
— James Allen

I LIVE IN Rich & Abundant Prosperity!

I have more than enough of everything
I need & desire and I GIVE GENEROUSLY!

Thank YOU Abba, for INCREASING my
CAPACITY for & EXPERIENCE of
WEALTH & PROSPERITY
far beyond my wildest dreams!

Thank YOU for USING ME in a powerful way
to INCREASE the LOVE, the JOY, the PEACE,
the POWER, and the PROSPERITY
in the lives of so many!

I AM the LOVE, the JOY, the PEACE, the POWER
& the PROSPERITY of GOD in EXPRESSION!

I RECEIVE BLESSINGS of PROSPERITY abundantly
and I GIVE GENEROUSLY to others.

Money flows to me & thru me
freely and easily and
I LOVE SHARING THE WEALTH.

My PROSPERITY MANAGEMENT SKILLS are dramatically
IMPROVED and I AM so GRATEFUL!

Thank YOU for DRAMATICALLY IMPROVING ALL of my
Gifts, Talents & Skills!

I Am a DIVINE INSTRUMENT fully available
to the INPOURING and OUTPOURING
of the LOVE, LIGHT & JOY of GOD.

I AM the LOVE of GOD in EXPRESSION!

I AM the LIGHT of GOD in EXPRESSION!

I AM the JOY of GOD in EXPRESSION!

THANK YOU for the CLARITY OF VISION
that is INCREASING in Me!

THANK YOU for USING ME as a
BEACON of LIGHT for others
who are seeking your Love.

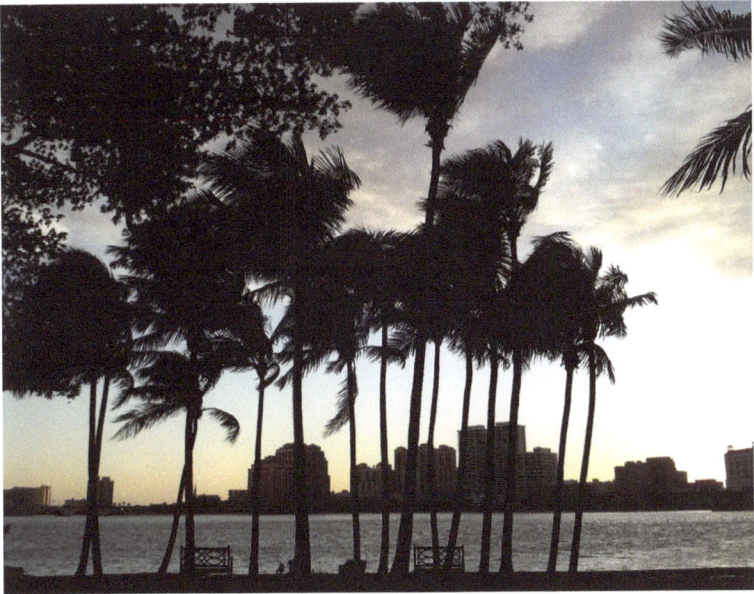

THANK YOU ABBA...THANK YOU AMMA
for So Many Wonderful Blessings!

Thank YOU for My LIFE, my HEALTH,
my Beautiful Loving FAMILY, my supportive
and loving FRIENDS, and the BEAUTY I see
all around my Neighborhood!

Thank YOU for the DRAMATIC IMPROVEMENT
in the QUALITY of My Life.

Thank YOU for the DRAMATIC IMPROVEMENT in
my Level of PROSPERITY and the
IMPROVED ABILITY to MANAGE IT ALL!

I AM the BEST Me I can BE!

I PRACTICE PROSPERITY PRINCIPLES daily and
I make AMAZING PROGRESS in the direction of
My DREAMS, DESIRES & GOALS.

I AM BLESSED & A BLESSING.

Thank YOU for making CLEAR the WAY to
UPLIFT, MOTIVATE, INSPIRE & EMPOWER
My SELF and OTHERS...
and for MANIFESTING the
TRUE DESIRES OF MY HEART!

I Ask for the ways & means to live a
Higher Quality of Life and God says YES!

I Seek God's Guidance and follow it Faithfully
to the fulfillment of
my Highest Purpose.

I Knock on the door of Love, Joy, Peace,
Wisdom & Prosperity and the
Windows of Heaven open wide and pour
Constant Miracles and
Opulent Blessings into my life!

Thank You God, for fulfilling your promises!

I Am a Winner in the Game of Life!

My Vision & Purpose are
Crystal Clear!

I see my Target clearly & take
One Step toward it daily,
no matter how small.

I trust God's all-giving Nature to
Direct me & Guide me step-by-step and
to Provide me with everything I need
to accomplish my goals.

I have the Faith to Believe and the
Patience to see it through to Success.

I Love & Appreciate the God in Me.

My Life Shines for ALL to see
the Love, Joy, Peace, Power & Prosperity
that Manifest thru God & Me.

Thank You for Using Me as a
Beacon of Light for Those who are
Seeking the Way to the
Kingdom of Heaven within!

GOD is OMNISCIENT—the Root of
All Knowledge, All Religion & All Science.

I see God's INTELLIGENCE & CREATIVITY in
All of Nature's Patterns.

God is the "Knower" in me,
therefore I have access to everything
I need to know when I need to know it.

THANK YOU for the flow of IDEAS & INSIGHTS
that unlock the Secrets of the Universe.

Thank you, Abba/Amma, for Blessing me
with DIVINE INTELLIGENCE,
SACRED KNOWLEDGE & WISDOM.

GOD is OMNIPRESENT—EVERYWHERE PRESENT.
There is No spot where God is Not;
Therefore GOD IS IN ME and I AM IN GOD.

GOD is OMNIPOTENT—ALL POWER,
the CREATIVE ENERGY that gives birth to
ALL of the Forces that Govern the UNIVERSE.

THANK YOU ABBA/AMMA
for PROVIDING all the ENERGY and RESOURCES
I need to carry out the
DREAMS & DESIRES You placed in my HEART.

THANK YOU for BEING the POWER that
GOVERNS my daily experience.

I Aᴍ Living at a Level of Fɪɴᴀɴᴄɪᴀʟ Fʀᴇᴇᴅᴏᴍ
Fᴀʀ Bᴇʏᴏɴᴅ Mʏ Wɪʟᴅᴇsᴛ Dʀᴇᴀᴍs!

I Aᴍ Experiencing a Gᴇɴᴇʀᴏᴜs &
Lᴜxᴜʀɪᴏᴜs Lifestyle Rɪɢʜᴛ Nᴏᴡ!

The Divine Pattern of
Lᴏᴠᴇ, Jᴏʏ, Pʀᴏsᴘᴇʀɪᴛʏ & Pᴇᴀᴄᴇ
flourishes Iɴ Mᴇ and Oᴠᴇʀғʟᴏᴡs
into the Lives of Those around me!

Sᴜᴄᴄᴇss & Mᴏɴᴇʏ are
drawn magnetically to me
and I sʜᴀʀᴇ the Wᴇᴀʟᴛʜ
Fʀᴇᴇʟʏ, Gᴇɴᴇʀᴏᴜsʟʏ, Aɴᴅ Hᴀᴘᴘɪʟʏ.

I have enough Time, Energy & Resources
to Do, Be & Have everything I desire!

Thank You for this Knowing,
for this Growing, and for this
Overflowing of Gratitude for
All that You Are In Me.

Thank You for Being the Love, the Joy,
the Beauty, the Peace,
the Power & the Prosperity that
pervade my Daily Existence!

I Love Life & Life Loves Me!

I AM GOD'S BELOVED!

GOD IS MY BELOVED!

I CLAIM my DIVINE INHERITANCE and RECEIVE the Blessings God has in store for me NOW.

I AM excited & delighted because
I AM experiencing record-breaking
FINANCIAL SUCCESS Right now!!!

I have MORE than enough
TIME, ENERGY, LOVE, MONEY & RESOURCES.

I AM filled with LOVE, JOY, & GRATITUDE!!!

Thank you GOD!!! Ashe!

THANK YOU, GOD for providing me with
EVERYTHING I NEED & DESIRE to live a
JOY-filled, PROSPEROUS LIFE.

My DREAM of having an OVERFLOW OF WEALTH
is now a REALITY & I generously donate
TIME, MONEY & RESOURCES to Worthy causes.

I Am surrounded by people who
LOVE, HONOR & RESPECT me and
I LOVE, HONOR & RESPECT
everyone around me.

I SURRENDER ALL thoughts of
fear, doubt & anxiety
to my Higher Power.

I open wide to RECEIVE the FAITH,
COURAGE & DETERMINATION that
FREE ME from All limitations.

THANK YOU for DRAMATICALLY IMPROVING
my FAITH in YOU and my FAITH in Me.

I welcome the SELF-ASSURANCE &
QUIET CONFIDENCE I feel
as I TRUST YOU more.

I AM ONE with my HIGHEST & BEST GOOD.

I AM a MESSENGER of LOVE, JOY, PEACE,
POWER & PROSPERITY for ALL!

I AM SO GRATEFUL to know that I have
ENOUGH OF EVERYTHING I NEED to be
HAPPY, HEALTHY & WHOLE!

My Conscious and Sub-Conscious Mind
work and play together in
DIVINE HARMONY to RE-CREATE my own
EXQUISITELY BEAUTIFUL UNIVERSE!

THANK YOU! THANK YOU! THANK YOU! Ashe!

THANK YOU for bringing my
PERFECTLY MATCHED PARTNER to me.

I AM LOVED and CHERISHED and I GIVE
LOVE, HONOR & RESPECT to my Loved One.

THANK YOU for the LOVING, JOYFUL,
HARMONIOUS, GOD-CENTERED and
MUTUALLY BENEFICIAL RELATIONSHIP we share.

We are BLESSED and a BLESSING to
each other, our family, and our community.

THANK YOU!

I AM A UNIQUE EXPRESSION OF GOD!

Thank you for helping me to
EMBRACE this TRUTH
every day and in every way!

Thank you for SHINING
the LIGHT of YOUR LOVE
IN, THRU & AS ME!

I AM SO GRATEFUL to BE in a
PLACE & SPACE of ACCEPTANCE of
WHO, WHAT & HOW I AM at
THIS time in my own EVOLUTION!

I see CLEARLY what I DESIRE to fulfill my BEING!
I ASK for IT and I GET IT!

I AM learning to ASK more WISELY.
I AM learning to LOVE with more
QUALITY and CONSISTENCY!
I AM learning to RESPECT & HONOR
my FEELINGS as well as my THOUGHTS.

I AM learning to HONOR & RESPECT my EMOTIONS
and how to TRANSCEIVE the
ENERGY and WISDOM that they bring.

THANK YOU ABBA! THANK YOU AMMA!

I face my fears with COURAGE,
FAITH & DETERMINATION to
RISE Above & Beyond to the
Next Level of My PERSONAL EVOLUTION!

My SPIRITUAL DEVELOPMENT is
Evident in my Daily Living.

My ABILITY & WILLINGNESS
to GIVE and to RECEIVE are
DRAMATICALLY IMPROVED!

Thank You Amma! Thank You Abba
for ALL of the BLESSINGS
IN, THRU & AS My LIFE!

HELP me to REMEMBER to TURN to YOU and
FOLLOW THRU in EVERY situation!

HELP me to INCREASE my
FAITH & TRUST IN YOU!

THANK YOU for ALL of the
GIFTS, TALENTS & SKILLS YOU Give to me.

THANK YOU for CLEARLY showing me the WAY
to share them with HUMANITY.

THANK YOU! THANK YOU! THANK YOU!

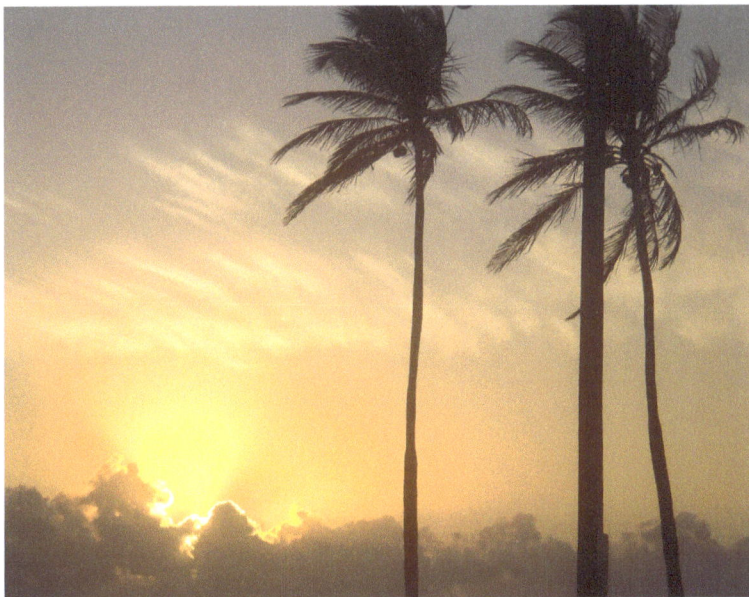

THANK YOU GOD! Thank You for BEING
the BREATH that BREATHES THRU ME!

THANK YOU for BEING the
RHYTHM that BEATS MY HEART.

THANK YOU for OPENING my EYES to SEE this
WONDERFUL REALITY that IS my LIFE
Right HERE on this BEAUTIFUL PLANET.

I AM EXPERIENCING the KINGDOM OF HEAVEN
Right HERE and right NOW!

THANK YOU for bringing my
PERFECTLY MATCHED PARTNER to me
and for the
LOVING, HARMONIOUS, GOD-CENTERED,
MUTUALLY BENEFICIAL RELATIONSHIP we Share.

All of my Relationships are filled with
LOVE, JOY, PEACE, FUN,
CARING, SHARING, GIVING & RECEIVING.

I AM SO GRATEFUL for ALL of the BLESSINGS
IN, THROUGH & AS MY LIFE.

Help me to LOVE with MORE
COMPASSION, QUALITY & CONSISTENCY.

THANK YOU GOD, for improving my ability to
GIVE LOVE and RECEIVE LOVE in both
Tangible & Intangible forms.

THANK YOU for HEALING
ALL of my RELATIONSHIPS and for helping me
to RELEASE everything that is unlike LOVE in
ALL ASPECTS of my LIFE.

I AM very GRATEFUL for so many
AWESOME GIFTS and BLESSINGS in my Life.

THANK YOU for the DRAMATIC IMPROVEMENT
in ALL of my GIFTS, TALENTS, & SKILLS.

THANK YOU for DRAMATICALLY IMPROVING
the QUALITY of my LIFE!

THANK YOU for BEING the LOVE, the JOY,
the PEACE, the POWER, and the PROSPERITY
that ARE MY LIFE NOW!

THANK YOU for LOVING ME and for
BLESSING ME SO Abundantly!

My FAITH & TRUST in GOD are GROWING.

I Know my BLISS comes in FOLLOWING THRU,
so I FOLLOW THRU on the GUIDANCE I receive
with FAITH, PATIENCE, PERSEVERANCE,
COURAGE & DETERMINATION!!

THANK YOU ABBA. THANK YOU AMMA for
INCREASING my ability to
RELAX & TRUST that
it IS YOUR GOOD PLEASURE to
FULFILL the DESIRES OF MY HEART.

I AM SO BLESSED and so GRATEFUL.

THANK YOU for ALL of the
AWESOME Blessings
YOU are showering into my Life!

THANK YOU for the BEAUTIFUL THOUGHTS,
PERCEPTIONS, ACTIONS and EMOTIONS
that ARE My Manifest Experience.

THANK YOU for SPEAKING CLEARLY,
LOVINGLY & POWERFULLY THRU ME!

THANK YOU for bringing the
DESIRES OF MY HEART FULLY into
MANIFESTATION in the HERE and NOW!

I AM STEPPING into MY HIGHER TRUTH.

I SURRENDER my small egoic self and
STEP INTO MY HIGHEST SELF!

THANK YOU for Bringing
PURE LOVE into the LIGHT of My Own Life!

I AM SO READY, WILLING & ABLE to
Step Up and Out into my
LARGER PLACE/SPACE to
CONFIDENTLY SERVE GOD.

PLEASE HELP ME to be CLEAR & CONFIDENT.

THANK YOU for LOVING ME & BLESSING ME!

My HIGHEST TRUTH carries me
forward into my BEST DESTINY!

I Am PERFECTLY ALIGNED Spiritually, Mentally,
Emotionally, and Physically
as I YIELD to the call of my SPIRIT.

I AM IN LOVE WITH LIFE!

LIFE IS IN LOVE WITH ME!

I AM a CONDUIT for the CREATIVE LOVE ENERGY that IS
the ALL of EXISTENCE!

I AM the LOVE of GOD IN ACTION!

I AM PERFECTLY ALIGNED with
GOD'S BLUEPRINT for my LIFE!

THANK YOU for OPENING Any and All
CIRCUITS within me that have previously
been closed or blocked in any way!

THANK YOU AMMA. THANK YOU ABBA for
HEALING my BODY, MIND & SPIRIT and
returning me to YOUR PERFECT PLAN.

THANK YOU for the LOVE that I GIVE
and for the LOVE that I RECEIVE!

I AM fully AVAILABLE to the UNCONDITIONAL LOVE
GOD expresses THRU ME!

I radiate JOY, PEACE, COMPASSION,
BEAUTY, POWER & PROSPERITY.

People are HEALED, UPLIFTED, MOTIVATED,
INSPIRED & EMPOWERED by the
PRESENCE of GOD they see in me.

THANK YOU GOD, for the QUALITY of LOVE
YOU GIVE ME & SHARE THRU ME.

# About the Author

Rev. Kalimba Love is the Co-Founder & Visionary Leader of Open Heart Ministry (OHM), an active force in Palm Beach County, Florida. She is a long-time friend & follower of Agape International Spiritual Center's founder, Rev. Michael Bernard Beckwith and his wife, Ricki Byars-Beckwith.

Since Kalimba's spiritual rebirth in December of 1975 she has been on a quest for Truth and Enlightenment. It is apparent to her audiences that she truly enjoys sharing insights she has gathered along her quite "colorful" spiritual path. Reverend Love has been opening hearts and minds with her music and entertaining teaching style since the early 1980's.

Kalimba has manifested many miracles in her life. She has faced and overcome many of life's toughest challenges and attributes her success to her faith in God and practicing Universal Laws. Always aspiring to help others learn to use these and other spiritual tools, she became a licensed Law of Attraction Practitioner and Spiritual Life Coach in 2012.

Sis. Kalimba Love and the OHM Family CommUnity, are on a mission to uplift, motivate, inspire & empower themselves, their Families and their Communities. In addition to working toward their VISION of opening a Family Empowerment Center, this group of Healing, Performing & Visual Artists offers various educational and entertaining programs that make a positive difference in the communities they serve. Their primary offering is Love...for God, for Self, for Family and Community.

To learn more about
- ❖ Kalimba Love
- ❖ Open Heart Ministry
- ❖ M.O.M.M.A. Mastermind Groups
- ❖ How to schedule a coaching session
- ❖ How to purchase other products
- ❖ or how to book Kalimba Love for your next event:

Visit our website: www.kalimbalove.com
Email: Ask@kalimbalove.com
Or Call:  561-582-7664

Other Products & Services from Kalimba Love:

- ❖ Audio/Music–
  "Meditations for Better Living"
  "Songs to Soothe Your Soul"
  "Celebrate the Light"
  "Heal My Soul"
  "God Is Love"
- ❖ Customized Inspirational Calendars
- ❖ Framed Inspirations
- ❖ Greeting Cards
- ❖ **M**indful **O**f **M**iracles **M**astermind **A**lliance™

www.ingramcontent.com/pod-product-compliance
Lightning Source LLC
Chambersburg PA
CBHW041225270326
41934CB00001B/3